WHEN TURTLES COME TO TOWN

WHEN TURTLES COME TO TOWN

BY CARY B. ZITER
Photographs by Chuck Bigger

Franklin Watts
New York / London
Toronto / Sydney
A First Book / 1989

Photographs courtesy of:
Chuck Bigger, except the following:
Adolph Gucinski/Monroe County
May Hill Russell Library: pp. 31, 33, 34, 35;
Florida State Archives: p. 36.

Library of Congress Cataloging-in-Publication Data

Ziter, Cary B.
When turtles come to town.

(A First book)
Bibliography: p.
Includes index.
Summary: A young child is filled with awe and wonder
at the arrival of sea turtles on a Florida beach near
his home.
1. Sea turtles—Florida—Juvenile literature.
2. Reptiles—Florida—Juvenile literature. [1. Sea
turtles. 2. Turtles] I. Bigger, Chuck, ill. II. Title.
III. Series.
QL666.C536Z58   1989   597.92   88-37843
ISBN 0-531-10691-8

Also by Cary B. Ziter

THE MOON OF FALLING LEAVES:
The Great Buffalo Hunt

*Special thanks to Rick Wolfe and
Bill Pyles of Boca Raton, Florida.
Their cooperation and professionalism
helped make this book possible.*

*Also, thanks to Norman Soule
for reading the manuscript.*

For my darling Joanne

WHEN TURTLES COME TO TOWN

INTRODUCTION

Every summer a wonderful drama unfolds on many sandy beaches hugging the Atlantic Ocean of the Southeast United States: sea turtles come ashore and lay their eggs. This is an important event. For years the great turtles were killed in large numbers, but now many people are involved in saving these harmless sea-going animals.

This is the story of how one boy and girl were lucky enough to meet experts involved in the gallant effort of preserving the still-shrinking sea turtle population. While reading about their adventure, you will learn a lot about these reptiles dating back 100 million years to the time of the incredible dinosaurs.

And who knows, someday you might vacation or live near the mighty, crashing ocean, making it possible for *you* to take part in something truly wonderful—that special moment when turtles come to town.

DIGGING FOR EGGS

The June heat surrounded the three people, thick and heavy as if a wool blanket covered them. It was only 8 A.M., but in Florida, it is often oven-hot from dawn until midnight.

The waves of the Atlantic Ocean, though, were nice and cool. Jesse ran through them as they slapped the sand. The water felt great swirling around his bare feet.

"Hurry up," Jesse called to his father and younger sister Claire, who were several steps behind him. They didn't hear him over the crash of the foaming sea. Jesse enjoyed running over the waterlogged earth, and he had a hard time holding back.

"Wait, Jesse, wait," cried Claire. The wet, mushy sand slowed her down.

Claire's daddy took her hand, and they soon caught up with Jesse. It was easy, because Jesse had suddenly

DAD, JESSE, AND CLAIRE RUN ALONG
THE BEACH IN THE EARLY MORNING.

stopped dead in his tracks. There was something strange
going on in front of him, something he had never seen
before on the beach. A big man, even taller than his
daddy, was standing in front of him. He had a bushy
beard, but Jesse knew it wasn't Santa Claus, especially
since old Santa couldn't take this heat after living in the
North Pole for so long. The man was digging in the
sand, his shirt was off, and his face was red from work-
ing so hard.

"Maybe he's looking for some treasure," Jesse whispered softly. "Anyway, I better not get too close."

The boy's father finally caught up to him. "Dad, what's he doing?" Jesse asked.

Jesse's father was out of breath, the sweat thick on his tanned forehead.

"I think he's digging up turtle eggs," he answered.

DAD, JESSE, AND CLAIRE COME UPON
RICK, CHIEF ENVIRONMENTAL
OFFICER IN BOCA RATON, FLORIDA,
WHO IS DIGGING UP A TURTLE NEST.

DAD POINTS OUT
TURTLE TRACKS.

Sand caked the arms of the man digging. He stopped
just long enough to nod in agreement. He too was hot
in the early morning sun. A steady stream of perspira-
tion rolled down his neck. While digging and counting,
he told Claire and Jesse that the female sea turtles swim
ashore every year during the summer months to lay their
eggs.

"I've got to move these eggs so they stand a better
chance of hatching. They're too close to the water. When

high tide comes, they may get washed away," said the bearded man. His name was Rick, and he was the chief environmental officer for Boca Raton, a small city about fifty miles north of Miami, Florida. Rick picked up an egg and let Jesse and Claire hold it for a few seconds. He warned the children not to turn the egg over, since this could lead to deformed hatchlings or dead eggs. Jesse appeared just a little afraid of the egg. He certainly knew it wouldn't bite or anything like that, but because it was an egg, he worried it might drop and break.

A PERFECTLY ROUND TURTLE EGG. ITS SHELL IS LIKE LEATHER.

"See, it's kind of like a ping-pong ball. They're just like a chicken egg inside, but the shell is like leather," Rick said.

The children discovered he was right, as they touched the egg. It really did feel like a leather coat someone would wear to fight off the chill of winter. They couldn't get over how perfectly round it was—Mother Nature showing she knows how to make beautiful things if just left alone to do the job.

Jesse suddenly ran off with Claire, racing over the sun-soaked sand, splashing through the dying end of a once-roaring wave. Several hours later, the children ate lunch at their house, only a few miles from the Florida coast.

"Say, Dad," Jesse asked unexpectedly, "when are we going to see the turtles?"

Jesse's father looked surprised. "How can we see the turtles, they haven't hatched yet."

The children's mom had a thought. "You can't see the baby turtles, but you can see the mother turtles. The city sponsors several turtle watches," she said, digging through a recent newspaper. She pointed to an article with a big color picture of a sea turtle surrounded by people. "See, you actually get to see the big female turtles laying their eggs. The only problem is that they come ashore very late at night."

"Can we go, Dad? Can we?" Jesse asked excitedly.

"Gee, it will be late and dark," Jesse's father said.

"Please, Dad," Jesse pleaded.

Claire joined in. "Please, Daddy, please."

Their father sighed, threw up his hands, and smiled. "OK, we'll go tomorrow."

Claire and Jesse each gave him a big hug. They couldn't wait to see the turtles. All day long, Jesse asked his mother the same question: "Has tomorrow come yet?" Jesse and Claire couldn't help being eager. Just thinking of seeing the big female sea turtles gave them a thrill.

It seemed like forever before the next day arrived, with night taking its time before rolling round. Although it was 9 P.M., Jesse was still wide awake. Not so for little Claire. Her father tried several times to wake her, but each time he did, she just smiled a little, closed her eyes again, and fell back asleep. So Jesse and his father left without her and drove a few miles to Boca Raton's Gumbo Limbo Nature Center which is operated by the Palm Beach County School System.

Rick was there when they arrived, along with Bill and Laurie, two other people who work with Rick in the city's effort to save and protect sea turtles. The nature center's small lecture hall was packed with people. Why were they so eager to learn more about sea turtles? Australian biologist Robert Bustard summed up the reasons nicely when he wrote, "Turtles have always fascinated people, partly because of the enormous size attained, partly because of their appearance—they are literally enclosed by a box or armored shell—but mainly, I suspect, because they are living dinosaurs."

Laurie stood before the group and started talking about turtles. She said the animals come ashore on the Boca Raton beaches from May to August to lay their eggs, almost always at night. Five of the world's seven species of sea turtles are found off Florida's coast: the Kemp's ridley, the hawksbill, the green sea turtle, and the leatherback, all on the endangered species list, and the loggerhead, which is considered threatened. The loggerhead is the most common turtle in Florida, one of the most important breeding areas for the species in the world.

While Laurie talked about the turtles, Rick left the nature center and went down to the beach. He plowed through the sand in total darkness on a three-wheel, motorcycle-like vehicle. His eyes were used to scanning the gray patches of darkness looking for turtle tracks without the help of lights.

"Turtle one to turtle two."

A walkie-talkie at Laurie's side crackled. The entire audience paid attention, the nature center suddenly as quiet as a church.

RICK, ON HIS THREE-WHEELER AT NIGHT,
LOCATES A TURTLE NEST AND RADIOS
BACK TO THE GROUP WAITING AT THE
GUMBO LIMBO NATURE CENTER.

"Come in, turtle one."

"OK, I've found one," Rick said, his voice a bundle of scratchy, distant sounds.

A big smile cut its way across Jesse's face, and like everyone else in the room, he became jumpy and eager. Laurie's eyes lit up as she and Bill told everyone how to get to the beach where Rick had found the turtle.

Jesse grabbed his father's hand and raced to their car. They drove less than a mile to the ocean. The other people from the lecture hall were there too. The moon hid behind the thick evening clouds. The night was sticky and warm as the crowd started walking down the beach. Waves slapped the shore, singing their wonderful song as Jesse and the forty people finally found Rick. They quickly surrounded the female turtle, who was already dropping her eggs.

"She's kind of in a dream state now," Rick explained as Jesse moved closer. Every single egg was perfectly round and as shiny white as the eggs you buy in the store. The turtle's nest was a big round pit in the ground dug by the turtle's powerful back flippers. The eggs dropped several inches, but none of them broke, thanks to their leather-like shell.

"We can talk, take pictures, do whatever we want. Nothing bothers her now," Rick said.

THE GROUP FROM THE NATURE CENTER WATCHES
AS RICK EXPLAINS THE LAYING PROCESS.

ABOVE: A CLOSE-UP LOOK AT THE TURTLE'S
HEAD SHOWS A PROTECTIVE TEAR SHED
AS THE TURTLE LAYS HER EGGS.
FACING PAGE: A CLOSE-UP VIEW OF THE EGGS
AS THEY DROP FROM THE BIRTH CANAL.

ABOVE: A REAR VIEW SHOWING THE TUR-
TLE'S FLIPPERS COVERING UP THE EGGS
AFTER THEY'VE BEEN LAID. *FACING PAGE:*
AS JESSE FOLLOWS AND WATCHES, THE
TURTLE RETURNS TO THE OCEAN AND RE-
ENTERS THE SURF AFTER COMPLETING
THE LAYING PROCESS.

AS A TURTLE SITS IN HER NEST, LIGHTS FROM
CONDOMINIUM APARTMENTS IN THE BACKGROUND
ARE VISIBLE. LIGHTS CAN CONFUSE THE TURTLE
HATCHLINGS IF THEY MISTAKE THE LIGHTS FOR
MOONLIGHT OVER THE OCEAN AND HEAD IN THE
WRONG DIRECTION.

Flash, flash, flash. A dozen cameras clicked as Laurie pointed toward the condos only a few dozen yards away. Condos are tall buildings with many apartments in them. Laurie said the city had asked condo owners and people in other buildings near the beach to dim their lights at night now that the turtles were coming. The lights confuse baby turtles hatching at night. Something inside them gives their brain a signal and tells them to head toward the moonlight high over the ocean. If they see a false light, the hatchlings sometimes think it's the moon. Instead of heading for the water, they head the wrong way. Beachfront light is responsible for the death of thousands of sea turtle hatchlings each year in Florida.

Flash, flash, flash. More pictures, but the mother turtle, her paddle-like flippers moving, ignored the intense camera light, even though it was as if bright stars were suddenly close enough for someone to reach out and touch. The people on the beach talked about how wonderful the turtle was and how important it was to keep animals such as this alive.

HUNTING, POACHING

Only recently, however, has the coming ashore of sea turtles sparked talk of saving them. Not so long ago, the event was seen as an easy opportunity to kill the shell-covered reptiles. In Florida, as in other coastal states in the southeastern part of America, sea turtles and turtle eggs were a main source of food for early pioneers who settled along the sandy beaches.

One woman who moved to Florida in 1894, for example, recalled that she and her friends often had picnics on the beach, and during a full moon, they hunted for turtles. The men would chase the animals just after they laid eggs, flipping the turtles over so that they were helpless.

"They returned the next day to butcher them and pass around the delicious steaks. While we were not particularly fond of turtle eggs, it was fun to hunt out the

KEY WEST BRAND

16 OZS. MEAT

GREEN TURTLE MEAT

PACKED BY THOMPSON FISH CO.,
KEY WEST, FLORIDA.

KEY WEST BRAND
GREEN
TURTLE MEAT
DIRECTIONS.

Make a broth as follows: Cut in pieces and put in a stock pot about three pounds of lean soup beef, salt and enough water to boil it in. Boil slowly and skim well, add some or all of the following: Carrot, Onions, Leek, one head Celery, Parsley; garnished with Bay Leaves, Thyme, Basil and Sage in proportion. One whole Pepper, Allspice, a few Cloves and one or two blades of Mace, all tied together in small cloth. Boil slowly two to four hours, and pass the broth through a fine strainer into a large tin pan, then add the Turtle Meat, cook until boiling hot, season with pepper and salt and serve. Or may be made into a delicious Meat Pie.

TURTLE MEAT WAS CONSIDERED A DELICACY UNTIL A FEDERAL LAW PUT TURTLES ON THE ENDANGERED SPECIES LIST. THIS CAN LABEL GIVES A RECIPE FOR TURTLE SOUP.

nest. The loggerhead often made false nests to fool bears and panthers who were particularly fond of the eggs, so we often dug into several turtle wallows before we found the real nest with its hundreds of soft-shelled eggs," the woman said.

Pioneer Charles Peirce, describing life in Florida in the 1870s, recalled that the turtle eggs were boiled, scrambled, put into pancakes, and used by bakers, but never fried since the white of a turtle egg doesn't get hard when cooked.

"The meat was good, something like poor beef when cooked properly," he said.

Hunting turtles became a big business. A man named Charles Parke managed to catch 2,500 turtles in 1886 with eight nets. He did his fishing in the Key West area. A total of 738 turtles weighing 36,900 pounds and valued at $2,722 were landed in this area in 1890. This number was caught by twenty-four men using 168 turtle nets.

This business came and went quickly in certain areas. In Tampa, for example, it was a lively trade in 1890, but by 1895, it was nearly dead. In Cedar Key, Florida, there were 113 nets in operation in 1890, but only 43 in 1895. Statewide, however, the trade hung on. In 1937, about 10,000 pounds of turtle were harvested, principally green turtles. In 1943, the number increased to 50,000 pounds, and in 1947, it went to 60,000 pounds.

UNLOADING A TURTLE BOAT. THE TURTLE
BUSINESS WAS A THRIVING ONE IN THE
LATE NINETEENTH CENTURY.

Even in the 1960s, a so-called turtle "corral" and
slaughterhouse still operated in Key West, Florida. For
years, Key West supplied 80 percent of all the turtle
products marketed in the United States. The animals'
skin made good leather products, their meat became a
steak or stock for soups, and their shells were made into
jewelry. One of these corrals is still standing. Next to the
slaughterhouse and cannery, a museum displays a 1,250-

A TURTLE CORRAL IN KEY WEST, FLORIDA

pound mounted sea turtle said to be the largest ever caught. There is even a grinder once used to make turtle burgers and a painting of the *A. Maitland Adams*, the last of the turtle schooners operating in the Florida Keys. When the boat returned to Key West after a turtle hunt, the docks were crowded with tourists eager to see the turtles pushed down ramps on their backs into the water-filled corrals. They were then roped by fishermen, and they had their flippers tied before being hauled to the slaughterhouse.

THE TURTLE SCHOONER *A. MAITLAND ADAMS*
BROUGHT ONE HUNDRED AND THIRTY-FIVE
LIVE GREEN TURTLES FROM HONDURAS TO
KEY WEST, FLORIDA, IN 1971, ON HER LAST
TURTLING TRIP.

LOGGERHEAD SEA TURTLES CAN WEIGH
300 POUNDS OR MORE. THIS ONE, CAUGHT
IN THE 1880s, WEIGHED 350 POUNDS.

The killing of sea turtles was legal in the United States until a federal law put the animals on the endangered species list. Following this action, state and local governments started programs dedicated to rebuilding turtle populations. These programs certainly saved some turtles and their eggs, but despite the widespread effort, the U.S. Fish and Wildlife Service estimated the population of loggerheads along the Atlantic coast declined about 4 percent a year. Worldwide, the number also continued to shrink, for many different reasons.

The human population explosion, which contributes to the loss of nesting habitats, is the main reason for the sea turtle population decline. Homes, condominiums, and office buildings now sit on the sand once considered prime nesting ground. This fight for land is not limited to states such as Florida. On Zakinthos, an island belonging to Greece, a debate has raged for years: should beaches be built on the golden sand? Each year, because of tourism or water pollution, the number of turtles returning to Zakinthos is reduced by about a fifth. Allowing more beachfront development certainly would reduce the turtle population even more.

Poachers take a number of eggs, too. Of course, there are the animal kingdom's natural poachers such as raccoons and foxes, but humans still do a lot of damage. In fact, certain coastal counties in Florida have been forced to create a marine patrol. This patrol protects the beaches from people who prey on turtle nests during the summer. Catching such criminals, who sell the eggs for about one dollar each, is not an easy task, however, when there are between 60 and 80 miles of beach to patrol each night in Palm Beach County alone.

Fishermen worldwide still kill many sea turtles—some by accident, some on purpose. Shrimp fishermen have no intention of killing turtles when they lower their nets. The turtles, however, get wrapped up in the fishing gear. Because they must surface for air, they accidentally drown. According to one study, about 12,000 sea turtles die this way each year, "enough to push these already imperiled creatures even closer to the brink of extinction."

Although these reptiles dating back 100 million years are protected in the U.S., some other countries allow unchecked slaughter. Consider Japan. This country alone imports more than 60,000 pounds of turtle shells a year for jewelry and eyeglass frames. That's a huge number of turtles, given that an average living loggerhead weighs about 300 pounds, with its shell only a part of its total weight.

FINDING A NEST

Jesse was unaware of all these worldwide environmental problems as he sat late at night near the female turtle and watched her lay dozens of eggs. He did, however, want to learn more about these creatures, who are so graceful and strong in the water, yet so clumsy and slow on land.

"Tell you what," Bill said to Jesse and his father as the turtle they watched with the rest of the crowd returned to the water. "I'll meet you early tomorrow on the beach. That will give you another chance to see how the eggs are found and moved to safety."

The next morning Jesse felt someone shaking him. First it was just a little shake, then a big one. Go away, go away, the boy thought to himself. His eyes felt glued together. There was more shaking. Finally, his eyes opened slowly and his father laughed.

"Are you going to jump out of that bed, you old hound dog?" the man chuckled. "You'd better, or we'll miss Bill moving the turtle eggs."

Jesse's father tried waking Claire while Jesse dressed, but, just like the night before, no matter what he did, she couldn't keep her brown eyes open. Jesse knew how she felt; staying awake was a big struggle.

So without Claire, they jumped in the car, meeting Bill on the beach a few minutes later. The sky was one long curtain of black, so dark the stars still twinkled brightly. The long stretch of sand was completely empty. The waves were very small, but like always, they sang a gentle, pleasant good morning.

"Listen," Bill said just before starting his three-wheeled vehicle. There was a yelping sound, something like a dog's bark, only higher pitched. Jesse took his father's hand, his eyes narrow with fear. In the darkness, the boy saw the outline of a small, pointy-eared animal.

"It's a gray fox," Bill explained, his smile broad and satisfied. "I can't get over it. It lives here in the park, and they're usually shy, but this one greets me every morning. It even comes within a few feet of me before turning and running away."

Varo-o-o-o-m. Bill turned the engine over. Three wheels chewed up the earth, and Bill moved toward the water. Up and down the beach he traveled. He soon discovered unusual markings in the sand.

BILL, WHO WORKS AT THE GUMBO LIMBO NATURE
CENTER, IS ON THE BEACH AT SUNRISE LOOKING
FOR THE NEST FROM THE PREVIOUS NIGHT.

"A false crawl," Bill explained, pointing to the sand
when Jesse and his father arrived. "Tracks, but no nest."
The shy turtle apparently came ashore, but something
spooked her as she searched for sand with the right mix-
ture of moisture and temperature. She re-entered the
water without laying eggs. A minute later, however, Bill
discovered the spot where she again came ashore.

"All right. I'll bet it's a real nest this time. A loggerhead too. I can tell by the tracks," he said.

Then he pointed to different marks in the sand a few feet away from the turtle nest. "See those," he asked, "a fox was here this morning and so were a couple of ghost crabs. They love to eat the turtle eggs."

Only a tiny number of turtle hatchlings reach adulthood—perhaps one out of a hundred. Raccoons, foxes, crabs, and birds are part of the animal society that feeds on eggs or baby turtles. Fish, too, eat them once the hatchlings reach the ocean.

A sound similar to the three-wheeled vehicle noise caught Bill's attention. It was a tractor moving toward the three people, although it was still several hundred yards away. Bill worked quickly. Standing over the place where the turtle tracks ended, Bill carefully poked the sand with a metal rod. He had a lot of experience, so he could tell by the way the sand felt that he had indeed discovered a nest. With his bare hands, he pushed the dirt aside quickly, but carefully.

ABOVE: THE TRACTOR THAT RAKES THE BEACH FOR DEBRIS AT DAWN. BILL MUST FIND THE TURTLE NESTS AND MOVE THEM BEFORE THE TRACTOR FINDS THEM. *BELOW:* BILL USES A SMALL STEEL ROD TO DETERMINE IF EGGS ARE IN THE NEST OR IF IT IS A FALSE CRAWL. THE TRACTOR IS IN THE BACKGROUND.

BILL DIGS UP A NEST OF
EGGS AS JESSE LOOKS ON.

Rays of sun finally started creeping through the many shades of gray clouds as the sound of the once-distant tractor grew louder. "The tractor driver tries to be careful, but if I don't get here early, some of the nests are ruined by accident when the tractor runs over them."

With the light still dim, Bill counted 132 eggs—a little higher than the normal clutch of about 100 eggs.

BILL EXCAVATING THE NEST. NOTICE
THE PERFECT ROUNDNESS OF THE EGGS.

Without turning them, he gently placed each of the white, perfectly round eggs in a large plastic pail and carried them further up the beach, stopping where the grass met the sand. (Moving turtle eggs is best left to professionals, as they have the experience and knowledge necessary to do this.) Then he dug another hole, making sure it was about as deep as the one he had just collected the eggs from. He buried the eggs and then placed a wire mesh cage over the spot. A sign identified the site as a turtle nest and warned beachcombers not to disturb it. In about fifty to sixty days, baby turtles would hatch, dig their way to the surface, and struggle toward the open sea.

Scientists aren't exactly sure what happens to little sea turtles once they reach the ocean and begin swimming furiously. Some researchers believe the hatchlings spend several years floating wherever the offshore current takes them on "rafts" of seaweed. These grassy life preservers are populated by many little fish, worms, and other tiny animals baby turtles feed on. From

THE BEACH-RAKING TRACTOR MAKES
ITS WAY AROUND A MARKED NEST
THAT WILL NOT BE RELOCATED.
THE SIGN ON THE NEST READS,
"TURTLE NEST, DO NOT DISTURB."

TOP: SEA TURTLE PROTECTION SPECIALIST DAVID
FARMER SETS UP WIRE CAGES THAT WILL HOUSE
RELOCATED NESTS IN THE HATCHERY. *BOTTOM:*
A VIEW INSIDE THE WIRE ENCLOSURE OF A NEST
THAT HAS HATCHED OUT.

A HATCHLING STILL TRAPPED IN PART
OF HIS EGG IS GIVEN A LITTLE HELP.

ABOVE: A LOGGERHEAD AND A LEATHERBACK HATCHLING SWIM AWAY AFTER ENTERING THE SURF. THE LEATHERBACK IS THE LARGER OF THE TWO. *FACING PAGE:* HATCHLINGS HEADING TO THE OCEAN AT DAWN. MOST OF THEM ARE LOGGERHEADS, BUT THERE IS AN OCCASIONAL LEATHERBACK IN THE GROUP.

hatchlings, the turtles grow to the size of a saucer as they drift thousands of miles around the globe, then to the size of a dinner plate, and finally, many years later and fully grown, they return to sandy beaches.

It is generally believed that despite years of drifting, despite feeding grounds hundreds or even thousands of miles away, female turtles, like the salmon fish, always return to the area where they were born to lay eggs. Trying to figure out how turtles live, biologists think they may have an answer to this mystery—turtles "smell" their way home.

"Researchers believe that tiny turtle hatchlings can imprint on distinct chemical characteristics of the beach and, years later when they reach breeding age, remember and retrace trails of these chemicals carried by ocean currents," said a report in the magazine *BioScience*.

A COMPARISON OF TWO YEARLINGS. AFTER ONE YEAR'S GROWTH, THE LOGGERHEAD (BOTTOM) AND THE LEATHER-BACK ARE CLOSER IN SIZE THAN WHEN THEY WERE HATCHED.

When Bill finished moving the first nest, he started searching for another, but Jesse's father said he had to leave. Jesse begged him to stay, but his father tossed up his hands and, with a sigh of frustration, said it was time for him to go to work.

The beach came alive a bit as Jesse and his father headed for the car. One person walked barefoot through the wet sand; a few seagulls spoke to each other in the distance; a boat sped over the foaming waves, heading directly into a staircase of clouds reaching toward the peek-a-boo sun.

TO RETURN NEXT YEAR

Jesse raced to find his mom when they entered the house. He chatted excitedly about the morning's events. Claire was now awake, attacking a big bowl of cereal as her father followed Jesse in and headed for the bedroom.

"Hey, how come you didn't wake me up?" she scolded.

"We tried waking you, honey, honest we did," her father said, searching his bedroom closet for a blue suit.

Claire asked all kinds of questions about the turtles, and Jesse showed off a little by answering many of them. A thought popped into Jesse's head, and he shouted to his father.

"I want to see a turtle again, Dad," the lad said.

"What's that, son?" his father answered, fixing his necktie in front of a mirror.

A YEARLING LOGGERHEAD SWIMMING
IN A TANK AT THE GUMBO LIMBO
NATURE CENTER. SOME HATCHLINGS
ARE KEPT BACK FOR A YEAR TO
INCREASE THEIR ODDS OF SURVIVAL
ONCE THEY ARE RELEASED.

Jesse thought about how uncomfortable the tight-fitting strip of cloth looked around his father's neck.

"The turtles, the turtles. I want to watch the turtles laying eggs again."

Jesse's father stopped what he was doing and came over to the boy. He put his arm around him. "Oh, yeah, don't worry. You'll get to see a turtle again, but we won't get to do it again until next year." The boy was excited. Next year, next year, he thought to himself, can I really wait that long?

The sun was high and beautiful as Jesse's dad left the house and slid into his car, this time in a fancy business suit instead of shorts and a baggy shirt. He beeped the horn and waved as he left for work. The boy waved back.

A minute later, Jesse found himself recalling his trips to the beach. The thoughts were grand ones, thanks to the wonderful sea creature and the great people he had met, and he kept thinking just how terrific it would be when summer rolled around again next year—that special moment when turtles come to town.

BIBLIOGRAPHY

Bustard, Robert. *Sea Turtles*. New York: Taplinger Publishing Co., 1972.

Carr, Archie. "Rips, Fads, and Little Loggerheads." *BioScience*, February 1986.

"Commercial Fishing Reducing Sea Turtle Numbers." *The Boca Raton News*, July 27, 1986.

"Congressmen vs. Sea Turtles." *The New York Times*, June 29, 1987.

Cox, Christopher. *A Key West Companion*. New York: St. Martin's Press, 1970.

"A Greek Drama: Tourists vs. Turtles." *The New York Times*, June 29, 1987.

Ingle, R. M., and F. G. Smith. *Sea Turtles and the Turtle Industry*. Coral Gables: University of Miami Press, 1970.

"The Misguiding Light: An Eco Soap Opera." *Discover*, December 1986.

Pierce, Charles W. *Pioneer Life in Southeast Florida*. Coral Gables: University of Miami Press, 1970.

Tangley, Laura. "Smelling Their Way Back Home?" *BioScience*, June 1984.

"Turtle Nesting Season Brings Back Beach Patrol." *The New York Times*, June 19, 1987.

Utz, Dolra Doster. "Life on the Loxahatchee." *Tequesta: The Journal of the Historical Association of Southern Florida*. 32 (1972).

"Wanted: Poachers of Turtles Eggs, Snook." *The Palm Beach Post*, July 6, 1986.

INDEX

ABOUT THE AUTHOR

Cary B. Ziter's literary repertoire
ranges from articles for newspapers
to scholarly journals to shoot-'em-up
cowboy stories to comedy. He is an
executive speechwriter for a major
multinational corporation and lives
with his family in Hong Kong.